THE GENE AUTRY CHRISTMAS BOOK

ISBN 978-1-4803-9506-0

7777 W. Bluemound Rd. P.O. Box 13819 Milwaukee, WI 53213

Visit Hal Leonard Online at
www.halleonard.com

It takes many talented folks to preserve, restore, and promote Gene Autry's musical legacy.
Thanks and appreciation goes to the following, who made *The Gene Autry Christmas Songbook* possible:

Autry National Center of the American West
Marva Felchlin, Director, Libraries and Archives
Manola Madrid, Research Services Associate

Gene Autry Entertainment
Mrs. Gene Autry
Tessa Blanchard, Music Research Assistant
Jocelyn Buhlman, Melody Ranch Radio Show Research Intern
Karla Buhlman, President
Holly George-Warren, Official Gene Autry Biographer
Maxine Hansen, Executive Assistant to Mrs. Gene Autry
Irynne Isip, Archival Assistant
Suzie Weston, Music Business Affairs

Audio Mastering and Restoration of Gene Autry's Melody Ranch Radio Show
by **Bob Fisher**/Pacific Multimedia Corporation

Gene Autry Photo Restoration by **Howard and Jill Levine**, CDS Photos & Graphics

Thanks also goes to Hal Leonard Corporation, including the following:
Mark Carlstein, Publication Editor
Ben Culli, Publication Editor
Jennifer Dzik, Designer
Linda Lemerond, Licensing Administrator
Jeff Schroedl, Executive Vice President
Nancy Ubick, Vice President, Business Affairs

For more information on America's Favorite Singing Cowboy visit www.geneautry.com

Cover, Gene Autry from his 1957 LP *The Original: Gene Autry Sings Rudolph the Red-Nosed Reindeer & Other Christmas Favorites*.

Introduction

America's Favorite Singing Cowboy, Gene Autry, was already a popular film and radio star when his connection to Christmas music began in 1942, after he enlisted in the United States Army Air Forces. His popular weekly radio show at the time, known as "Sergeant Gene Autry," was broadcast nationwide on the CBS Radio Network. On his November 8th and December 20th shows, Gene sang Bing Crosby's holiday hit "White Christmas." Every December after World War II until Gene's "Melody Ranch Radio Show" ended in the mid-1950s, Gene continued to perform this song, although he never recorded "White Christmas" for commercial release.

Returning to his entertainment career in 1946, Gene was the Grand Marshal of the annual Santa Claus Lane Parade in Hollywood, California. Several floats behind him was Santa Claus in his sleigh. While riding his famous horse, Champion, along the route, Gene heard the excited children chanting "Here comes Santa Claus! Here comes Santa Claus!" These words, along with the clip-clop of Champion's hooves, inspired the song "Here Comes Santa Claus (Right Down Santa Claus Lane)." Gene co-wrote the song that winter with Oakley Haldeman, songwriter and Vice President of Gene Autry's Western Music Publishing Company, and it was released on Columbia Records on October 6, 1947. "Here Comes Santa Claus" became an instant hit. Gene performed it live on his radio show every holiday season from 1947 through 1955. "Here Comes Santa Claus" is also the only Christmas song Gene performed on the silver screen, in his 1949 film *The Cowboy and the Indians*.

In 1949, songwriter Johnny Marks had unsuccessfully pitched his song, "Rudolph the Red-Nosed Reindeer" to several recording artists, including Perry Como, Bing Crosby, and Dinah Shore. Gene, looking for his next holiday hit, was encouraged by his wife Ina and his musical arranger Carl Cotner, to record "Rudolph the Red-Nosed Reindeer," and the song was released on Columbia Records on September 1st with "If It Doesn't Snow on Christmas" on the flipside. That October Gene sang "Rudolph" live on his radio show for the first time. The song became so popular that, outside of his signature theme song "Back in the Saddle Again" and the Western classic "Tumbling Tumbleweeds," Gene performed "Rudolph" more than any other song on his radio shows and tours. Gene's recording became a multi-million seller heard around the world and into the twenty-first century.

By the 1950s, Gene was known not only for his movie, television and radio career but also for his Christmas music. To keep the holiday hits coming, Gene collaborated with Oakley Haldeman on "Santa, Santa, Santa"; and with Johnny Marks on "When Santa Claus Gets Your Letter," "Everyone's a Child at Christmas," and "Nine Little Reindeer." Gene also sang with other recording artists, such as Rosemary Clooney on "Look Out the Window (The Winter Song)"; and with the Mitchell Choirboys on "Where Did My Snowman Go?" While the girl group, The Pinafores, provided the backing vocals on his 1949 Christmas recordings, it was the Texas-based trio, The Cass County Boys, who accompanied Gene on his hits of the 1950s including "Frosty the Snow Man" and "The Night Before Christmas, In Texas That Is." By this time, Gene's original fans from the 1930s and 1940s were now parents, so several holiday songs like "Poppy the Puppy"; "Hardrock, Coco and Joe (The Three Little Dwarfs)"; "I Wish My Mom Would Marry Santa Claus"; and "Santa's Coming in a Whirlybird" were aimed at a younger audience.

Since many of these songs have been out of print and hard to find—some available in print here for the very first time!—this unique collection gives folks the opportunity to sing and play Gene Autry's Christmas classics with their friends and family, and perhaps rekindle that holiday spirit, creating new memories for the next generation.

Karla Buhlman
President,
Gene Autry Entertainment

US
ARMY
Holiday Greetings
FROM
GENE AUTRY
AND CHAMP

CBS
CBS

U.S.

GENE AUTRY SINGS
RUDOLPH, THE RED-NOSED REINDEER
AND
IF IT DOESN'T
SNOW ON CHRISTMAS
COLUMBIA RECORDS

Merry Christmas, Folks

BUON NATALE
(Means Merry Christmas to You)

Words and Music by BOB SAFFER
and FRANK LINALE

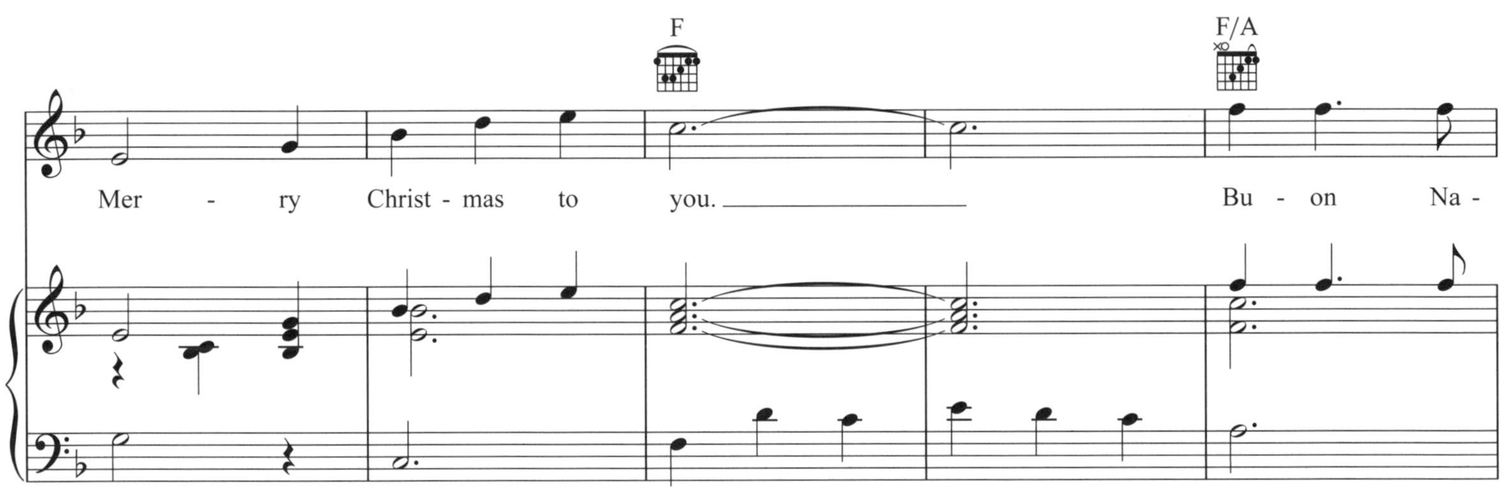

F6
F
F♯dim7
C7
lots of fun. Bu - on Na - ta -
F
le, may all your wish - es come true.
F/A
G♯dim7
C7
Bu - on Na - ta - le in It - a - ly means a
To Coda
F
Mer - ry Christ - mas to you. Far a -

C7
F
way, a - cross the sea in
F6
F♯dim7
C7
sun - ny It - a - ly, there's a
Gm7
C7
Gm7
C7
quaint lit - tle town; not a clock has been wound for
Gm7
C7
C7♯5
8fr
F
o - ver a cen - tu - ry. They don't

C7
F
know the time or year, and
F6
F♯dim7
C7
Gm7
no one seems to care. And this is the
C7
Gm7
C7
Gm7
C7
rea - son the Christ - mas sea - son is cel - e - brat - ed all
F
C7
D.C. al Coda
year, oh!
CODA
F
you.

EVERYONE'S A CHILD AT CHRISTMAS

Music and Lyrics by
JOHNNY MARKS

C7♯5
F
Dm7
8fr
child at Christ - mas and
G7
C
F
C
G7
loves the hap - py hol - i - day jol - li - ty.
C
F♯dim7
G7
You must al - ways be - lieve that on
C
G7
Gm6
A7
D7
3fr
each Christ - mas Eve Old San - ta

Am7
D7
G7
Gdim7
Dm7
G7
Claus will be com - ing be-cause you're good, did ev - 'ry-thing you should.
C
C7♯5
8fr
F
Ev - 'ry - one's a child at Christ - mas,
Dm7
G7
for Christ - mas is for chil - dren like you and
1
C
G7
C6
G
F
Em
G7
me.
2
C
G7
C
me.
3

FROSTY THE SNOW MAN

Words and Music by STEVE NELSON
and JACK ROLLINS

F F♯dim7 C/G F F♯dim7
fair - y tale, they say; he was made of snow, but the
broom - stick in his hand, run - ning here and there, all a -
C/G A Dm7 G7 C C7
chil - dren know how he came to life one day. There
round the square, say - in', "Catch me if you can." He
F F♯dim7 C/G A7 Dm7 G7 C
must have been some mag - ic in that old silk hat they found, for
led them down the streets of town right to the traf - fic cop, and he
G G♯dim7 Am7 D9 4fr G G7♯5
when they placed it on his head he be - gan to dance a - round. Oh,
on - ly paused a mo - ment when he heard him hol - ler, "Stop!" For

C C7 F F#dim7 C/G
Fros - ty the Snow Man was a - live as he could be, and the
Fros - ty the Snow Man had to hur - ry on his way, but he
F F#dim7 C/G A Dm7 G7 C
chil - dren say he could laugh and play just the same as you and me.
waved good - bye say - in', "Don't you cry, I'll be back a - gain some - day."
G7
Thump - et - y thump thump, thump - et - y thump thump, look at Fros - ty go.
lightly
C
Thump - et - y thump thump, thump - et - y thump thump, o - ver the hills of snow.

HARDROCK, COCO AND JOE
(The Three Little Dwarfs)

Words and Music by
STUART HAMBLEN

E♭7 A♭ F7 B♭7

all a - bout San - ta and his help - ers three. There's Hard - rock and
you'll hear their laugh - ter, that much I do know. 'Twill be Hard - rock and

E♭ 𝄋 E♭ E♭7 A♭

Co - co and Joe. Now Hard rock's the driv - er up there by his
Co - co and Joe. The three lit - tle men, on - ly two feet
San - ta will come in and set down his

F7 B♭7 E♭ A♭ E♭

sleigh, Co - co reads maps and he shows him the way. Tho'
high, sing - ing to San - ta 'way up in the sky,
pack; and Hard - rock will hold the rein - deer till San - ta comes back. And if

E♭7 A♭ F7 B♭7

old San - ta real - ly has no need for Joe, but takes him 'cause
laugh - ing and shout - ing as the sleigh - bells ring, it's Hard - rock and
you hear a gig - gle as he turns to go, it's Co - co, a

E♭

he loves him so.
Co - co and Joe.
snow - ball and Joe.

O lee o lay dee, o

B♭7 E♭ A♭/E♭ E♭

lay dee i ay, Don - ner and Blitz - en, a - way, a - way.

A♭ Fm7♭5 E♭/B♭ B♭7

O lee o lay dee, o lay dee i o, I'm Hard - rock, I'm Co - co, I'm
(he's) (he's) (he's)

E♭ E♭7 A♭ E♭

Joe. And San - ta is bus - y with his heav - y

mf

A♭
E♭
F7
B♭7
E♭
pack. He trusts his driv - ers and nev - er looks back. O lee o
p
A♭
Fm
E♭/B♭
B♭7
To Coda
lay dee, o lay dee i o, I'm Hard - rock, I'm Co - co, I'm
(he's) (he's) (he's)
1
E♭
B♭7
2
E♭
B♭7
D.S. al Coda
CODA
E♭
Joe. Now Joe. And old
Joe.
B♭7
E♭
pp slowly

HE'LL BE COMING DOWN THE CHIMNEY
(Like He Always Did Before)

Words and Music by FRED COOTS
and AL NEIBURG

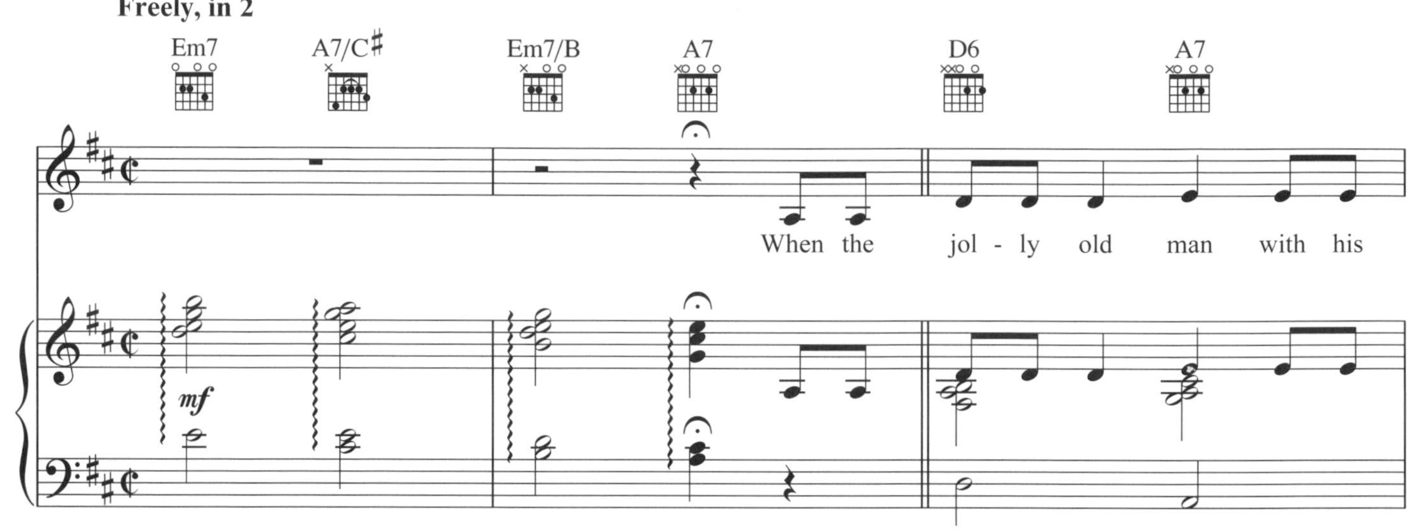

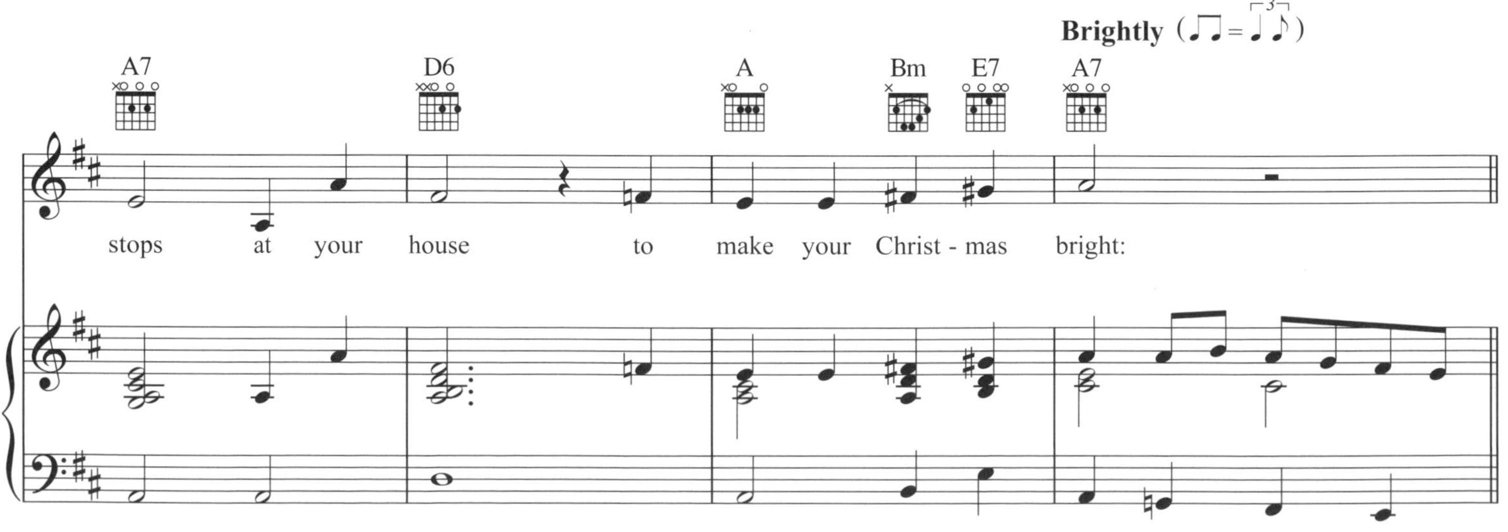

D6
Em7
Don't look out the win - dow, and don't wait by the door.
A7
D♯dim7
A7/E
D♯dim7
He'll be com - in' down the chim - ney, like he
A7
D6
al - ways did be - fore.
When you hear his
Em7
sleigh bells, don't look front or back.
He'll be

A7
D♯dim7
A7/E
D♯dim7
A7
com - in' down the chim - ney with a sack up - on his
D6
G
Em7
back. If you wrote your let - ter to
D6
Bm
Bm/A♯
7fr
San - ta, and you're good, you'll find your stock - ings
Bm/A
Bm/G♯
Em
Em7
A7
all filled up with the things you hoped you would. So,

D6
Em7
don't look out the win - dow, and don't wait by the door.
A7
D♯dim7
A7/E
He'll be com - in' down the chim - ney,
D♯dim7
A7/E
D♯dim7
yes, by gosh, by jim - i - ny, he'll be com - in' down the
A7/E
D♯dim7
A7
1
D6
2
D6
chim - ney, like he al - ways did be - fore.
fore.

HE'S A CHUBBY LITTLE FELLOW

Words and Music by GENE AUTRY
and OAKLEY HALDEMAN

C G+ C Em/B Am C
3fr
deer. He's a hap - py lit - tle fel - low with a pack on his back and a
day. If all you kid - dies will try your best to
year. If you hang up your stock-ings and be qui - et as a mouse and be
toys. So if you're good to your mom and dad and
C7 F A7/E Dm F6 F♯dim7
smile that shines so bright. He's the jol - ly lit - tle fel - low called
do ev - 'ry - thing just right, then the jol - ly lit - tle fel - low called
sure to turn off the lights, then the jol - ly lit - tle fel - low called
say your pray'rs each night, then the jol - ly lit - tle fel - low called
1–3
4
C/G E7 A7 C♯dim7 G7 C G+ C
San - ta Claus who'll be 'round on Christ - mas Eve night. He's a
San - ta Claus will be 'round on Christ - mas Eve night. He's a
San - ta Claus will be 'round on Christ - mas Eve night. He's a
San - ta Claus will be 'round on Christ - mas Eve night.

HERE COMES SANTA CLAUS
(Right Down Santa Claus Lane)

Words and Music by GENE AUTRY
and OAKLEY HALDEMAN

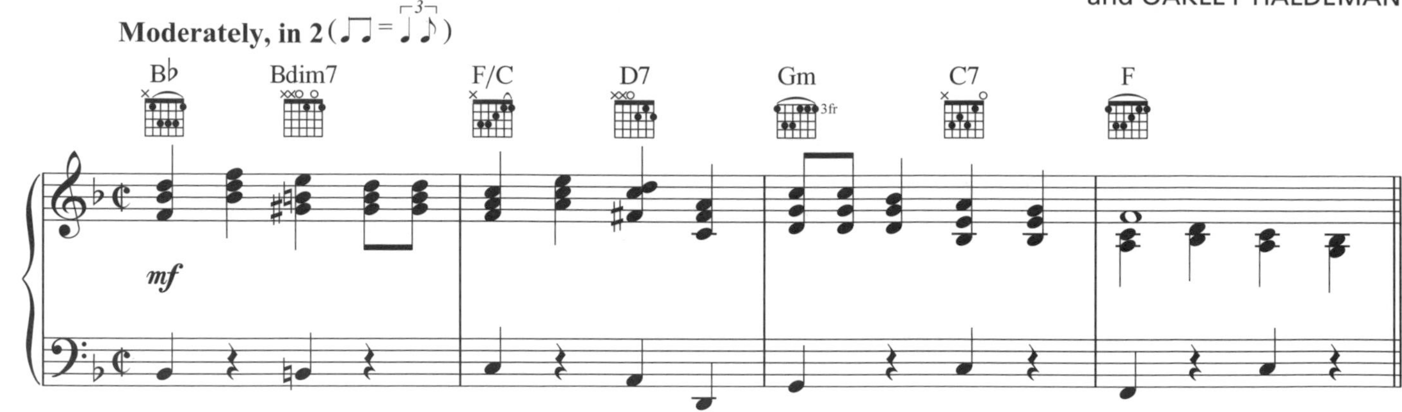

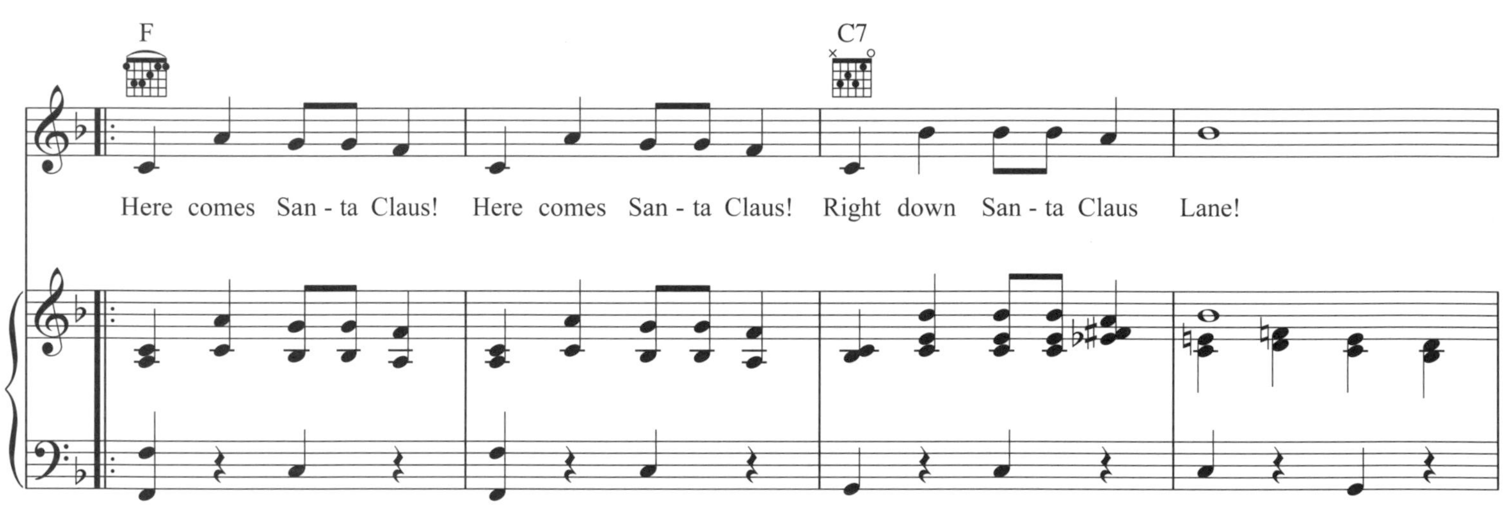

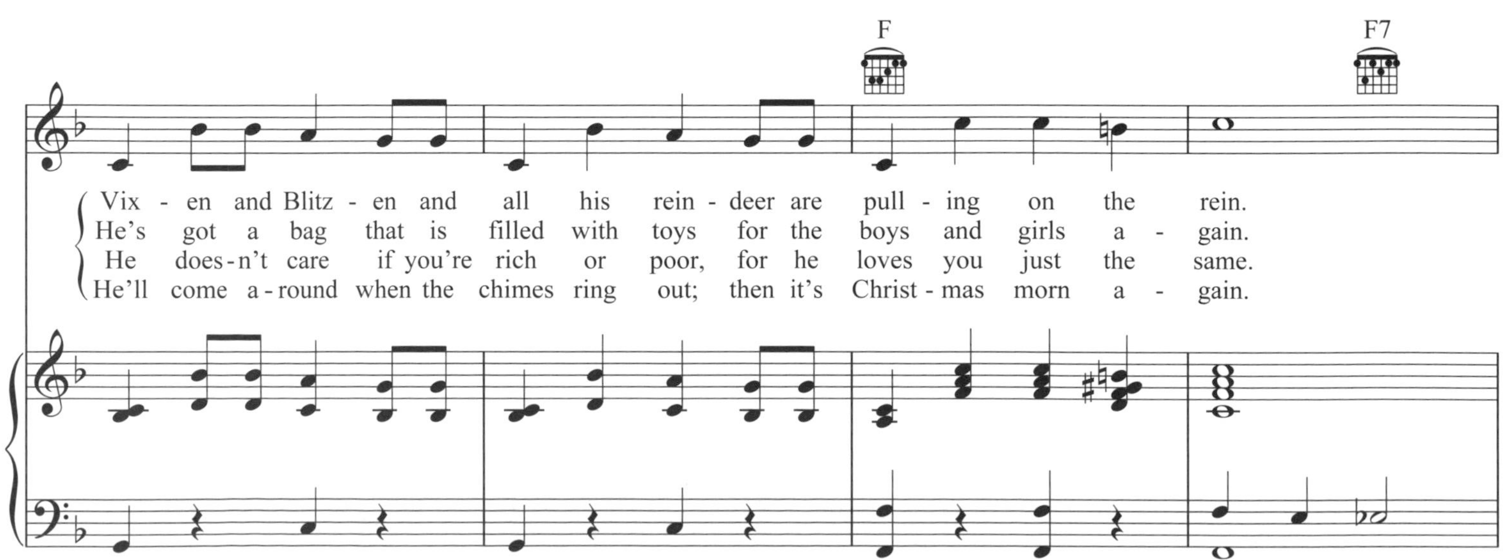

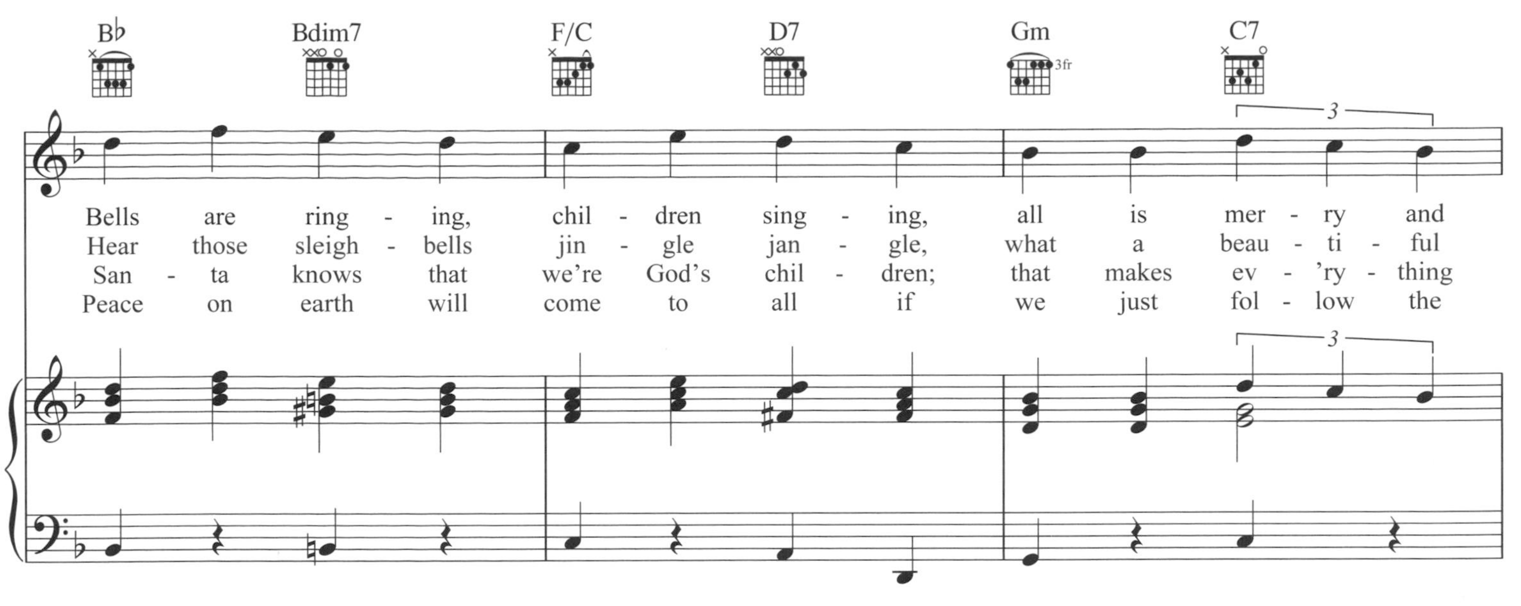
B♭
Bdim7
F/C
D7
Gm
C7
Bells are ring - ing, chil - dren sing - ing, all is mer - ry and
Hear those sleigh - bells jin - gle jan - gle, what a beau - ti - ful
San - ta knows that we're God's chil - dren; that makes ev - 'ry - thing
Peace on earth will come to all if we just fol - low the

F
B♭
Bdim7
F/C
D7
bright. Hang your stock - ings and say your pray'rs,
sight. Jump in bed, cov - er up your head,
right. Fill your hearts with a Christ - mas cheer,
light. Let's give thanks to the Lord a - bove,
'cause

1–3
Gm
C7
F
C7sus
San - ta Claus comes to - night.
4
Gm
C7
F
San - ta Claus comes to - night.

I WISH MY MOM WOULD MARRY SANTA CLAUS

Words and Music by GENE AUTRY
and MICHAEL CARR

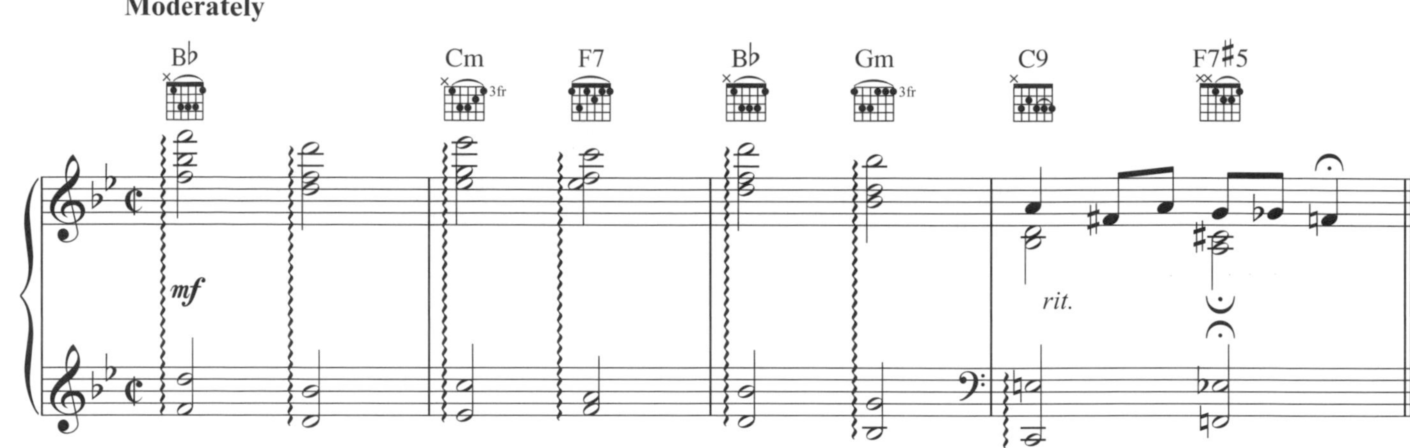

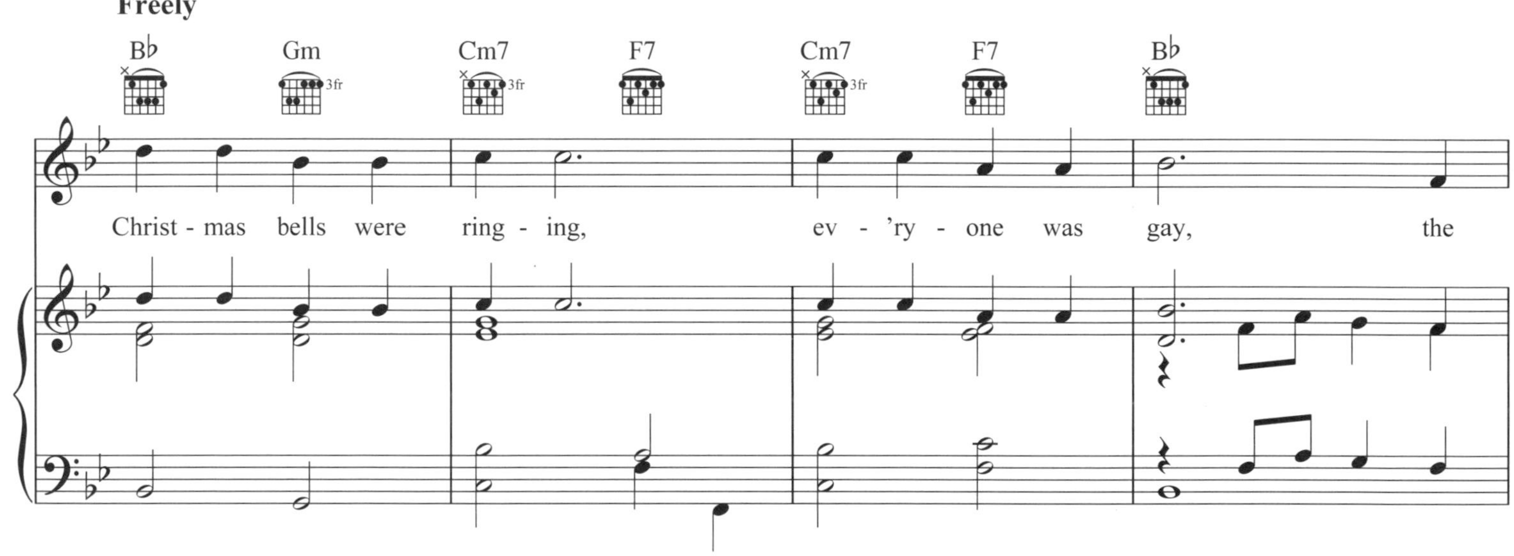

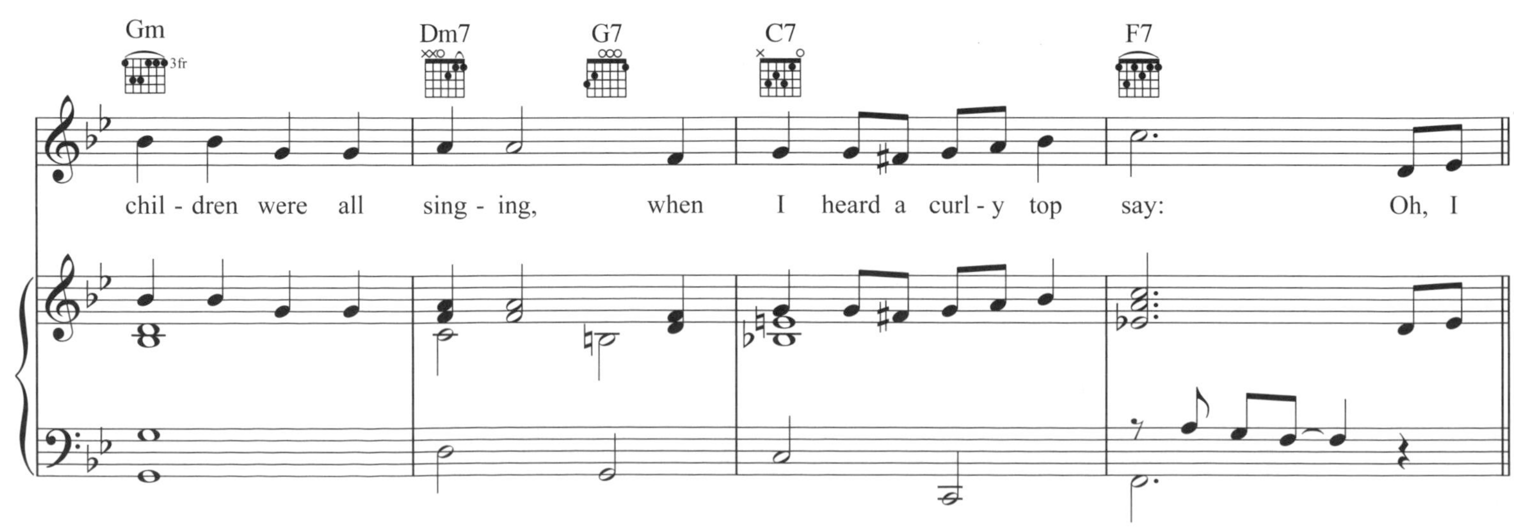

Medium soft-shoe
B♭
Gm7
C7
wish my mom_ would mar-ry San-ta Claus;_ then he'd be in the fam - i - ly.
F7
Gm
Cm7
F+
I'd like him 'round, you see, to help to dec-o-rate the Christ-mas tree. I
wish my mom_ would mar-ry San-ta Claus;_ then I know he would al-ways stay,
E♭m
Fm7
B♭7
and we could al-ways play with toys I get on Christ-mas day. All the year I know he's ver-y

Fm7 B♭7 B♭+ E♭6 Gm7 C7
bus - y shin - ing Ru - dolph's nose up bright. May - be I could help him keep it
Gm7 C7 F7 B♭
shin - y for that ver - y im - por - tant night. Oh, I wish my mom _ would mar - ry
B♭ Gm7 C7 Gm7 C7 F7
San - ta Claus; _ then he'd stay in the fam - i - ly, and it would al - ways
3
B♭ E♭m 6fr
1
B♭ D♭dim7 F7/C 3fr
2
B♭
be like Christ - mas ev - 'ry day for me. Oh, I me.

MERRY CHRISTMAS WALTZ

Words and Music by BOB BATSON
and INEZ LOEWER

B♭
A
B♭
ring - in' clear - er and clear - er,
C7
F
E
bring - ing Christ - mas near - er and
F
near - er. Mu - sic play - ing, cou - ples sway - ing, what a
C7
beau - ti - ful sight and the sea - son is the

F
rea - son we're so hap - py to - night. So
B♭
stay in my arms, dar - lin', keep sing - in'
F
C7
too. Mer - ry Christ - mas, mer - ry Christ - mas to
1
F
you. While we're
2
F
B♭m/F
F
you.
rit.

IF IT DOESN'T SNOW ON CHRISTMAS

Words and Music by GERALD MARKS
and MILTON H. PASCAL

F
C7
F
C7
F
just one lit - tle thing that wor - ries me:
If it
B♭
B♭maj7
B♭6
B♭
B♭maj7
does - n't snow on Christ - mas, how is San - ta gon - na use his
B♭7
E♭6
Gm
3fr
A7
sleigh? In case of rain, will there be a train that - 'll
B♭
G7
C7
F7
B♭
B♭maj7
speed him on his way? If it does - n't snow on

B♭6 B♭ B♭maj7 B♭7
Christ - mas, how will San - ta get a - round to us? If
E♭6 Gm A7 B♭ Cm F7
he breaks down on his way to town, will they let him use a
B♭ F7 F7♯5 B♭
bus? I've sent him a nice long let - ter, and I
A7 Dm C7
hope it's not in vain. I'd real - ly feel much
3fr

F
C7
F7
bet - ter if I knew he could fly a plane. Peo - ple
B♭
B♭maj7
B♭6
B♭
B♭maj7
say he has eight rein - deer for the sleigh he's driv - in'
B♭7
E♭6
Gm
3fr
here, but how'll he go if it does - n't snow on
C7
F7
1
B♭6
2
B♭6
B♭
Christ - mas this year? If it year?

LOOK OUT THE WINDOW
(The Winter Song)

Words and Music by LEW PORTER
and MITCHELL TABLEPORTER

D7
G7
Gdim7
G7
win - ter, it's win - ter - time a - gain.
C
(Harmony part small notes)
Look out the win - dow, look out the win - dow, see the snow - flakes
G7
fall. Look out the win - dow, look out the win - dow,
C
win - ter's come to call. Chil - dren sing - ing,

G7
sleigh - bells ring - ing, as they glide a - long.
Look out the win - dow, look out the win - dow, sing - ing the win - ter
C
F
song. Out there where the snow - man stands
C
F
on the i - cy lawn, chil - dren run to

D7
G7
shake his hands, for when the sun shines he'll be gone.
C
Hur - ry, hur - ry, see the flur - ry, win - ter won't last
G7
long. Look out the win - dow, look out the win - dow,
1
C
G7♯5
sing-ing the win - ter song.
2
Dm7
G7
C
sing-ing the win - ter song.

THE NIGHT BEFORE CHRISTMAS, IN TEXAS THAT IS

Words by LEON A. HARRIS, JR.
Music by BOB MILLER

E♭ E♭7 A♭ Fm
sleep in their cab - in were Bud - dy and Sue, a -
driv - er was "Gee" - in' and "Haw" - in' with will. And
burst in the cab - in, the chil - dren a - woke and were
E♭ Cm7 F7 B♭7 E♭
dream - in' of Christ - mas, like me and you. Not
hors - es, not rein - deer, he drove with such skill. "Come
both so as - ton - ished that nei - ther one spoke. And he
B♭ E♭
stock - in's, but boots at the foot of their bed, for
on, Buck and Pon - cho and Prince, to the right. There'll
filled up their boots with such pres - ents ga - lore that
B♭ F7/C F7 B♭7
this was in Tex - as. What more need be said? When
be plen - ty trav - 'lin' for you all to - night." The
nei - ther could think of a sin - gle thing more. When

E♭
E♭7
A♭
Fm
all of a sud - den, from out the still night there
driv - er, in Le - vi's and a shirt that was red, had a
Bud - dy re - cov - ered the use of his jaws, he
E♭
1, 2
Cm7
F7
B♭7
E♭
Fm
came such a ruck - us, it gave me a fright.
ten - gal - lon Stet - son on top of his head.
asked in a
E♭
Cm7
F7
B♭7
E♭
And I
As he
3
Cm7
F7
B♭7
E♭/B♭
E♭
B♭
whis - per, "Are you San - ta Claus?" "Am I the real

E♭
Cm
B♭
San - ta? Well, what do you think?" And he smiled as he
F7/C
F7
B♭7
E♭
gave a mys - te - ri - ous wink. Then he leaped in the
E♭7
A♭
Fm
E♭/B♭
buck - board and said in his drawl, "To the chil - dren of
Freely
Cm
F7/C
B♭7
E♭
E♭6
Tex - as, Mer - ry Christ - mas, you all!"

NINE LITTLE REINDEER

Words and Music by GENE AUTRY,
JOHNNY MARKS and MERLE TRAVIS

B7
E7
rein - deer took his place __ to bring the chil - dren joy on Christ - mas
A7
D
day. With one lit - tle, two lit - tle, three lit - tle rein - deer,
Instrumental
A
D
four lit - tle, five lit - tle, six lit - tle rein - deer, sev - en lit - tle, eight, yes,
A7
D
eight lit - tle rein - deer pull - in' San - ta's sleigh. Here's

A
Dash - er! Danc - er! Pranc - er! Vix - en! Com - et! Cu - pid! Don - ner! Blitz - en!
Hey, Santa! Look who's comin'!
D A7 D
But there's one lit - tle rein - deer miss - in', Ru - dolph is his name. For a
I'm Rudolph, the red-nosed reindeer! "It's
G Em7 D A7 D
long, long time, he had hitched up nine to make his Christ - mas ride. Now
been a year since we've been here, and how the time it goes. Where
G Em7 D E7 A7
Ru - dolph's gone, he's so a - lone, San - ta Claus sat down and cried. With
have you been, my lit - tle friend?" "Shin - ing up my nose!" There's

D
A
one lit - tle, two lit - tle, three lit - tle rein - deer, four lit - tle, five lit - tle, six lit - tle rein - deer,
D
1
A7
D
sev - en lit - tle, eight, yes, eight lit - tle rein - deer pull - in' San - ta's sleigh.
2
A
F♯m7
B7
Freely, in 4
Em
B7
nine lit - tle rein - deer pull - in' San - ta's sleigh. Peace on earth, good
In 2
Em
C♯7
A7
D
will to all, and a ver - y mer - ry Christ - mas day!

POPPY THE PUPPY

Written by TOMMY JOHNSTON

Fm7 B♭7 E♭
though he's just a lit - tle pup, he's fun - ny as a clown.
B♭7
Pop - py the pup - py hops up on San - ta's sleigh. He
Fm7 B♭7 E♭7
helps him load his pack of toys, then barks, "We're on our way."
A♭ E♭/G Cm7 Fm7 B♭7 E♭
Pop - py holds the rein - deer's reins be - tween his fluff - y paws, while

F7 B♭ Gm7 C7 F7sus F7 B♭ E♭
3fr
climb-ing down the chim-ney goes good old San-ta Claus. Pop-py the
B♭7
pup-py loves lit-tle girls and boys. He checks the list, you
Fm7 B♭7
1
E♭ B♭7
2
E♭
won't be missed. You'll get your share of toys. toys.
B♭7 E♭6
Hap-py lit-tle, pep-py lit-tle, fun-ny lit-tle, cute lit-tle Pop-py the pup-py.

ROUND, ROUND THE CHRISTMAS TREE

Words and Music by
FRED STRYKER

Dad - dy, there's your watch and chain. Grand - pa's got a
Aun - tie's got a new boy - friend. Broth - er's bike is
Bb7
Eb
Ab
brand - new cane, round the Christ - mas tree. Sis - ter, there's your
just the end, round the Christ - mas tree. There's a gift for
Eb
eve - ning gown. Tom, your ted - dy bear.
Un - cle Joe, some - thin' he can wear.
Cm
Cm/B
Cm/Bb
Cm
Fm
Adim
San - ta sure was good to us, left pres - ents ev - 'ry -
Look - y, here's what Grand - ma got, an eas - y rock - ing
3fr
4fr
3fr
3fr
8fr
8fr
3fr

F7
B♭7
E♭
3fr
where.
chair.
Round, round the Christ - mas tree, gath - er round the
Christ - mas tree. Let's all sing so mer - ri - ly,
1
B♭7
E♭
3fr
round the Christ - mas tree.
2
B♭7
round the
E♭
3fr
A♭
4fr
E♭
3fr
Christ - mas tree.

RUDOLPH THE RED-NOSED REINDEER

Music and Lyrics by
JOHNNY MARKS

A tempo
Bb
Bb/D
Dbdim7
Ru - dolph the red - nosed rein - deer had a ver - y shin - y
F7
nose, and if you ev - er saw it,
F7#5
Bb
you would e - ven say it glows. All of the oth - er
Bb/D
Dbdim7
F7
rein - deer used to laugh and call him names.

They nev - er let poor Ru - dolph join in an - y rein - deer
Bb
Bb7
Eb
3fr
Bb
Bbmaj7
games. Then one fog - gy Christ - mas Eve,
Cm
3fr
F7
Bb
Bdim7
F/C
San - ta came to say, "Ru - dolph, with your
Fmaj7
F♯dim7
Gm7
C7
F7
nose so bright, won't you guide my sleigh to - night?"

B♭
B♭/D
D♭dim7
Then how the rein - deer loved him, as they shout - ed out with
F7
glee: "Ru - dolph the red - nosed rein - deer,
1
B♭
F9
F7♭9
you'll go down in his - to - ry!"
2
F7/C
3fr
Bdim7
you'll go down in
F7/C
3fr
F7
B♭
Cm7
3fr
F7
B♭
his - to - ry!"

SANTA, SANTA, SANTA

Words and Music by GENE AUTRY
and OAKLEY HALDEMAN

E♭
and shout all day. Christ - mas time comes
for us to play. Let's be mer - ry,
E♭7 A♭
once a year, so let's all laugh and cheer. 'Cause
let's be gay and sing and shout all day that
Fm7 B♭9 E♭ Gm7♭5 C7 F7 B♭7
San - ta, San - ta, San - ta is on his way, hur - ray, hur - ray, hur - ray!
San - ta, San - ta, San - ta is com - ing to - night, hur - ray, hur - ray, hur - ray!
E♭ A♭
With his rein - deer eight, he might be late 'cause
With his love for kids, both rich and poor, he

Eb
Eb7
Ab
he's got lots to do. But don't you wor - ry, he'll be 'round to
treats us all a - like. He'll bring with him so man - y things,
F7
Bb7
Eb
Ebmaj7
Eb6
Eb
bring good things for all of you. Old San - ta, San - ta, San - ta is com - ing to - night to a
skates and trains and dolls and bikes. Old San - ta, San - ta, San - ta is com - ing to - night, oh,
Eb7
Ab
C7/G
Fm
Fm7
Bb7
Eb
Gm7b5
C7
world so bright and gay. So let's all sing and shout to him, hur - ray,
what a Christ - mas day. 'Cause San - ta, San - ta, San - ta will soon be here, hur - ray,
F7
Bb7
1
Eb
Cdim7
Bb7
2
Eb
hur - ray, hur - ray!
hur - ray, hur - ray!

SANTA'S COMING IN A WHIRLYBIRD

Words and Music by
ASHLEY DEES

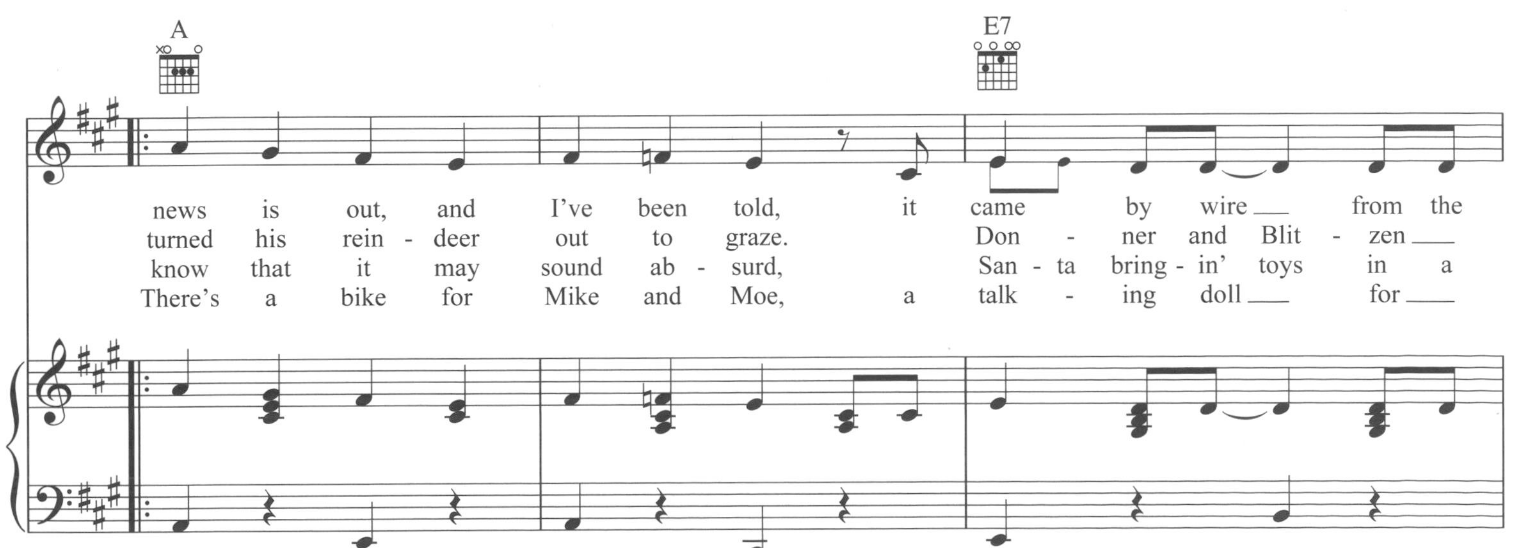

A
great North Pole. I'm sure each boy and girl - y heard,
were a - mazed. But Ru - dolph said with a hap - py shout,
whir - ly - bird. But he's been check - in' with the U. S. Mail, and
Jane and Jo. There'll be toys for ev - 'ry child, if you
E7
A
San - ta Claus has got a new whir - ly - bird.
"I'll go with San - ta and help him out."
with a hel - i - cop - ter he can't fail.
prom - ise not to drive Mom and Dad - dy wild.
San - ta's com - in' in a whir - ly - bird,
E7
Christ - mas night in a
A
whir - ly - bird.
So if you're good and you don't goof, the

1–3
E7
A
whir - ly - bird's gon - na land on your roof. (Whir - ly - bird, whir - ly - bird, whir - ly -
E7
bird, whir - ly - bird, San - ta's com - in' in a
4
A
whir - ly - bird.) He I on your roof. (Whir - ly -
A
E7
Repeat and Fade
Optional Ending
A
bird, whir - ly - bird, whir - ly - bird, whir - ly - bird, whir - ly - bird.)

SLEIGH BELLS

Words and Music by GENE AUTRY
and MICHAEL CARR

G7
Dm
jing jing jin - gl - ing, Christ - mas trees a - glow,
G7
hol - ly and mis - tle - toe and the whit - est kind of
C
C7
F
snow. All the kid - dies are sleep - ing, as
C
D7
he rides through the sky. But there must be no

G G♯dim7 D7 G7
peep - ing or he might pass you by.
C G7
Sleigh bells jin - gl - ing, jing jing jin - gl - ing, San - ta's on his
Dm G7
way. Hear the sleigh bells say, "A
1
C
hap - py Christ - mas day."
2
C A♭7 Dm7 G7 C
4fr
hap - py Christ - mas day."

THIRTY-TWO FEET, EIGHT LITTLE TAILS

Words and Music by JOHN REDMOND, JAMES CAVANAUGH and FRANK WELDON

Moderately bright

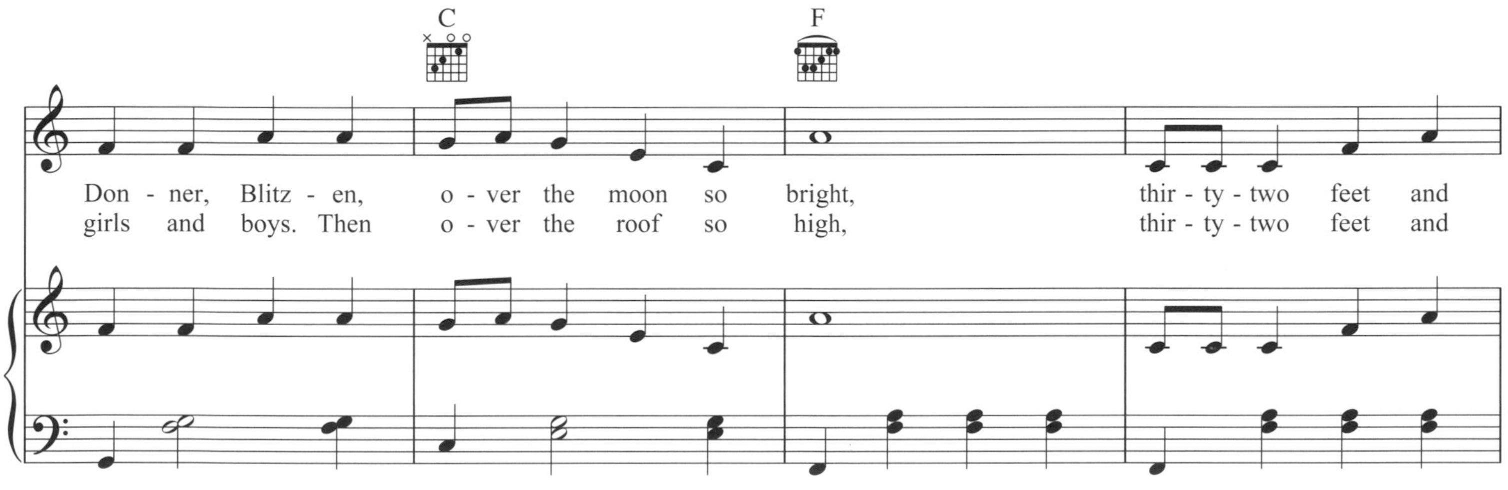

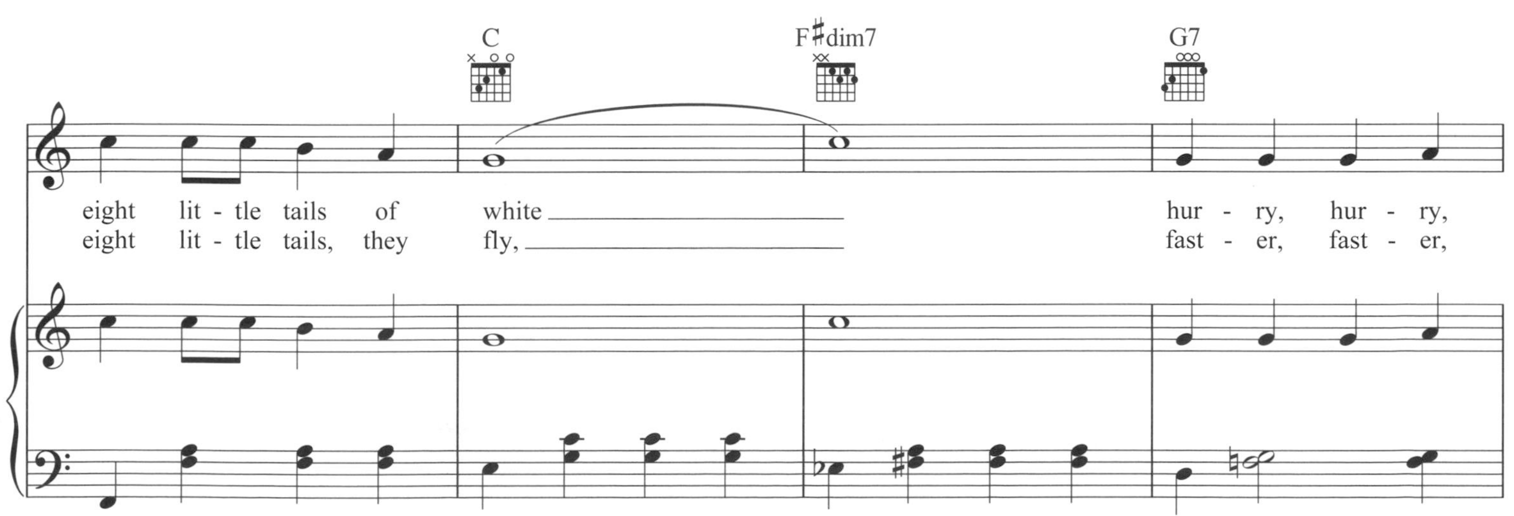

1
C
G7
2
hur - ry through the night.
fast - er through the
C
Dm7
E♭dim7
C/E
F
sky.
Oh!
Look at 'em
C/E
G7/D
C
D7
go,
San - ta laugh - in', "Ho, ho, ho, ho,
G7
C
ho, ho, ho, ho, ho."
Dash - er, Danc - er, Pranc - er, Vix - en,

G7
C
F
Com - et, Cu - pid, Don - ner, Blitz - en, o - ver the gar - den wall,
C
F♯dim7
thir - ty - two feet and eight lit - tle tails and all.
G7
A7
G/B
Cm
3fr
A7/C♯
See 'em can - ter, hear ol' San - ta call,
G7
C
"Mer - ry, mer - ry Christ - mas to you all."
cresc.
f

UP ON THE HOUSE TOP
(Ho! Ho! Ho!)

Words and Music BENJAMIN HANBY
Arranged by CARL COTNER

F
C/E
Dm
G7
C
all for the lit - tle ones, Christ - mas joys.
one that can o - pen and shut its eyes.
whis - tle and ball and a whip that cracks.
C7/E
F6
Dm7
G7
Ho! Ho! Ho! Who would - n't go! Ho! Ho! Ho!
C
C7/E
Who would - n't go! Up on the house top, click, click, click,
F
C
Dm
G7
C
down through the chim - ney with old good Saint Nick.
3

F6
C/E
Dm
G7
C
Play 4 times
C7/E
F6
Dm7
G7
Ho! Ho! Ho! Who would - n't go! Ho! Ho! Ho!
C
Who would - n't go! Up on the house top,
C7/E
F
C
Dm
G7
C
click, click, click, down through the chim - ney with good Saint Nick.

WHEN SANTA CLAUS GETS YOUR LETTER

Music and Lyrics by
JOHNNY MARKS

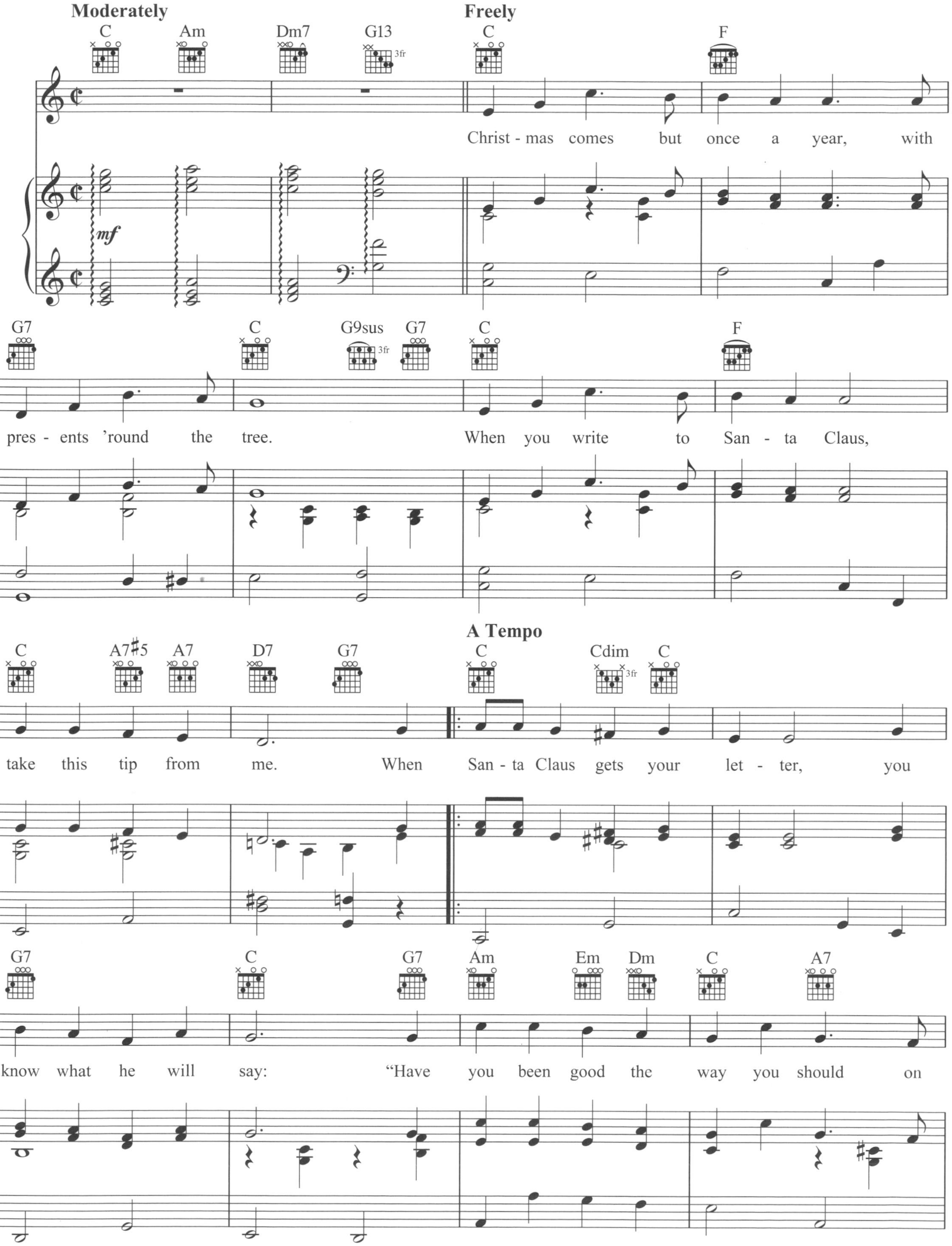

Moderately **Freely**

C Am Dm7 G13 C F

mf

Christ - mas comes but once a year, with

G7 C G9sus G7 C F

pres - ents 'round the tree. When you write to San - ta Claus,

A Tempo

C A7♯5 A7 D7 G7 C Cdim C

take this tip from me. When San - ta Claus gets your let - ter, you

G7 C G7 Am Em Dm C A7

know what he will say: "Have you been good the way you should on

D7
G7
G13
3fr
C
Cdim
3fr
C
ev - 'ry sin - gle day?" When San - ta Claus gets your let - ter, to
G7
C
G7
Am
Em
Dm
C
A7
ask for Christ - mas toys, he'll take a look in his good book he
D7
G7
C
C7
F
B7
keeps for girls and boys. He'll stroke his beard, his eyes will glow and
C
Cdim
3fr
C6
C7
F
E♭dim
6fr
at your name he'll peer; it takes a lit - tle time, you know, to

D7 G7 G13 C Cdim C
check back one whole year! When San - ta Claus gets your let - ter, I
G7 C G7 Am Em Dm C A7
real - ly do be - lieve, you'll head his list, you won't be missed by
D7 G7 1 C G9sus G13 2 C
San - ta on Christ - mas eve. When eve.
Am Dm7 G7 C

WHERE DID MY SNOWMAN GO?

A♯dim7 G/B G7 C F C G7
I can see his pipe and top - hat as they
gone to vis - it Ru - dolph, help - ing
C F C C♯dim7 Dm7 C♯dim7
lie there in the snow. Where did my snow - man,
San - ta through the snow? Where did my snow - man,
Dm7 C♯dim7 Dm7 G7 C C♯dim7 G7
where did my snow - man, where did my snow - man go? I've been
where did my snow - man, where did my snow - man go? I have
C F C G7 C F
ask - ing Mom and Dad - dy, but they said they did - n't
sent a note to San - ta. I am sure that he would

C
C#dim7
Dm7
C#dim7
Dm7
C#dim7
know. Where did my snow - man, where did my snow - man,
know. Where did my snow - man, where did my snow - man,
Dm7
G7
C
C7
F
where did my snow - man go? On - ly yes - ter - day I
where did my snow - man go? When I left him stand - ing
C/G
Am9
5fr
B♭dim7
met Jack Frost, he said, "There'll be a storm." So I
on the lawn, he seemed so cold and damp. I went
D7
G7
F/A
A#dim7
lit a lit - tle fi - re just to keep my snow - man
right in - to the house and got a nice, warm sun - ray

G7
C
F
C
G7
warm. Did he slide back home to Snow - land to be -
lamp. I would give a mil - lion pen - nies if he'd
C
F
C
C♯dim7
Dm7
C♯dim7
come an Es - ki - mo?
come back to me now.
Where is my snow - man?
Dm7
C♯dim7
1
Dm7
G7
C
C♯dim7
G7
Now there is no man. Where did my snow - man go? Has he
2
Dm7
C♯dim7
Dm7
G7
C6
Where did my snow - man go?

WHITE CHRISTMAS

Words and Music by
IRVING BERLIN

Fm6/C
G7/B
F/A
G7/B
Cmaj9
But it's De - cem - ber the twen - ty - fourth,
C6
Am6/E
B7/D♯
A/C♯
B7/D♯
and I am long - ing to be up
Em
Dm7
F/G
G7
C6
Dm/C
C
B/G
C/G
north.
I'm dream - ing of a
Dm7
F♯/E
G/F
F
white Christ - mas, just like the

G7
C
C6
F/G
G7
ones I used to know,
where the
C
Cmaj7
C9
F
Fm6
tree - tops glis - ten and chil - dren lis - ten to
C/G
F/G
C/G
D7
Dm7/G
G7
hear sleigh bells in the snow.
C6
Dm/C
C
B/G
C/G
Dm7
F♯/E
G/F
I'm dream - ing of a white Christ - mas

F G7 C
with ev - 'ry Christ - mas card I write:
F/G G7 C Cmaj7 C9
"May your days be mer - ry and
F Fm C/G Gdim7 F/G G7
bright and may all your Christ - mas - es be
1 C C/E Dm7 G7
white."
2 C Dm7/G C
white."

YOU CAN SEE OLD SANTA CLAUS
(When You Find Him in Your Heart)

Words and Music by LEFTY FRIZZELL, JOE JOHNSON and BOB ADAMS

G
Em7
D
starts.
You can see old San - ta Claus when you
smile.
You can see old San - ta Claus, for he's
Em7
A7
D
G
D7
find him in your heart.
been there all the while.
Though you may have a
G
D
A7
D
G
D7
Christ - mas where the snow will nev - er fall,
if you'll find him
G
D
E7
A7
D
in your heart, old San-ta's sure to call.
So keep look - in'

D7
G
Em7
for his rein - deer when Christ-mas sea - son starts. You can see old
D
1
Em7
A7
D
San - ta Claus when you find him in your heart.
G
Em7
D
A7
D
There's
2
Em7
A7
D
G
Em
D
find him in your heart.